What Can You Do With A... Scribble?

31 DAYS OF CREATIVE

RELAXATION, PERSPECTIVE & COMPASSION

WENDY FORD

2020

Grab your pencil and get ready to draw!

What is a scribble and what can you do with it?

Well, for the next 31 days we have created series of activities that will help push your imagination, creativity and perception of what an ordinary scribble might be. It is our hope that through these fun silly pages you will find that wonder and excitement can come from sometimes the most simple things.

What is my goal as the reader?

Over the next month make a little time each day to break out your pencils and your favorite coloring tools to complete the scribble puzzles we started. Turn those basic scribbles into your own artwork masterpieces! Don't worry if you think you are not creative. We know you have a great imagination and we will provide you clues along the way.

I have finished all 31 days of activities, now what?

That's easy, start again! The best part about this book is you can do these daily activities over and over. See what great new places your imagination will take you to. Use your daily scribble time to relax from life's stresses while building compassion for yourself and others, as you may struggle in a drawing. Finally, realize that stepping back and seeing something simple from a new perspective might show you the beauty that was always there.

WHAT IS A SCRIBBLE?
A SCRIBBLE CAN BE ANYTHING YOU IMAGINE.

TRY DRAWING WHAT YOU IMAGINE YOU SEE!

DAY 1

USING JUST A SCRIBBLE YOU CAN BE AN ASTRONAUT FLOATING THROUGH A CLOUD OF SPACE DUST.

CAN YOU SEE IT IN YOUR OWN DRAWING?

DAY 2

YOUR IMAGINATION CAN TURN YOU INTO A FISHERMAN FIGHTING OFF A HUGE SEA MONSTER ABOUT TO SWALLOW YOU WHOLE!

LOOK OUT BELOW!!!
(AS YOU COMPLETE THE PICTURE)

DAY 3

HAVE YOU EVER IMAGINED YOURSELF AS AN EXPLORER LOOKING THROUGH DARK CAVES FOR SPOOKY HIDING CREATURES?

I THINK I MAY SEE COUPLE YOU MIGHT BE ABLE TO DRAW HIDING BEHIND THOSE ROCKS.

DAY 4

WITH JUST A SCRIBBLE SOMETIMES I PICTURE MYSELF AS A CHUBBY DRAGON THAT HAS EATEN WAY TOO MUCH CAKE.

DRAW HOW SILLY DO I LOOK?

DAY 5

DAY 6

HAVE YOU EVER IMAGINED BEING A SMALL BUG WALKING THROUGH A GIANT GARDEN OF FLOWERS?

WHEN I SEE THESE SCRIBBLE I FEEL THAT WAY.

DAY 7

SOMETIMES IN A SCRIBBLE YOU MIGHT SEE SOMETHING DIFFERENT THEN THOSE AROUND YOU. IN THIS SCRIBBLE YOU MIGHT SEE A ___________ (ANIMAL) JUMPING THROUGH A RING OF ___________ (NOUN).

DAY 8

DAY 9

I HAVE BEEN TOLD THAT WITH A GOOD IMAGINATION
IDEAS CAN SNEAK UP ON YOU LIKE A SNAKE
MOVING THROUGH THE TALL GRASS.

DO YOU THINK THAT IT IS TRUE IN THIS DRAWING?

DAY 10

WOW! HAVE YOU EVER SEEN SUCH A LONG TAIL
ON A ______________.
(MYTHICAL CREATURE)
I KNOW YOU WILL BE ABLE TO IMAGINE
AND DRAW SOMETHINGLIKE THAT.

DAY 11

A STRONG IMAGINATION MIGHT HAVE MANY AMAZING THINGS BUZZING AROUND IN YOUR HEAD ALL AT ONCE.

DON'T YOU THINK GREAT IDEAS WORKING TOGETHER LIKE BUSY BEES CAN MAKE WONDERFUL THINGS HAPPEN?

DAY 12

SEEING THE WORLD THROUGH SOMEONE ELSE'S PERSPECTIVE CAN HELP YOU BETTER UNDERSTAND OTHERS AND HELP YOUR IMAGINATION GROW.

WHAT DO YOU THINK A FISH SEES AS IT LOOKS OUT THROUGH THE FISHBOWL?

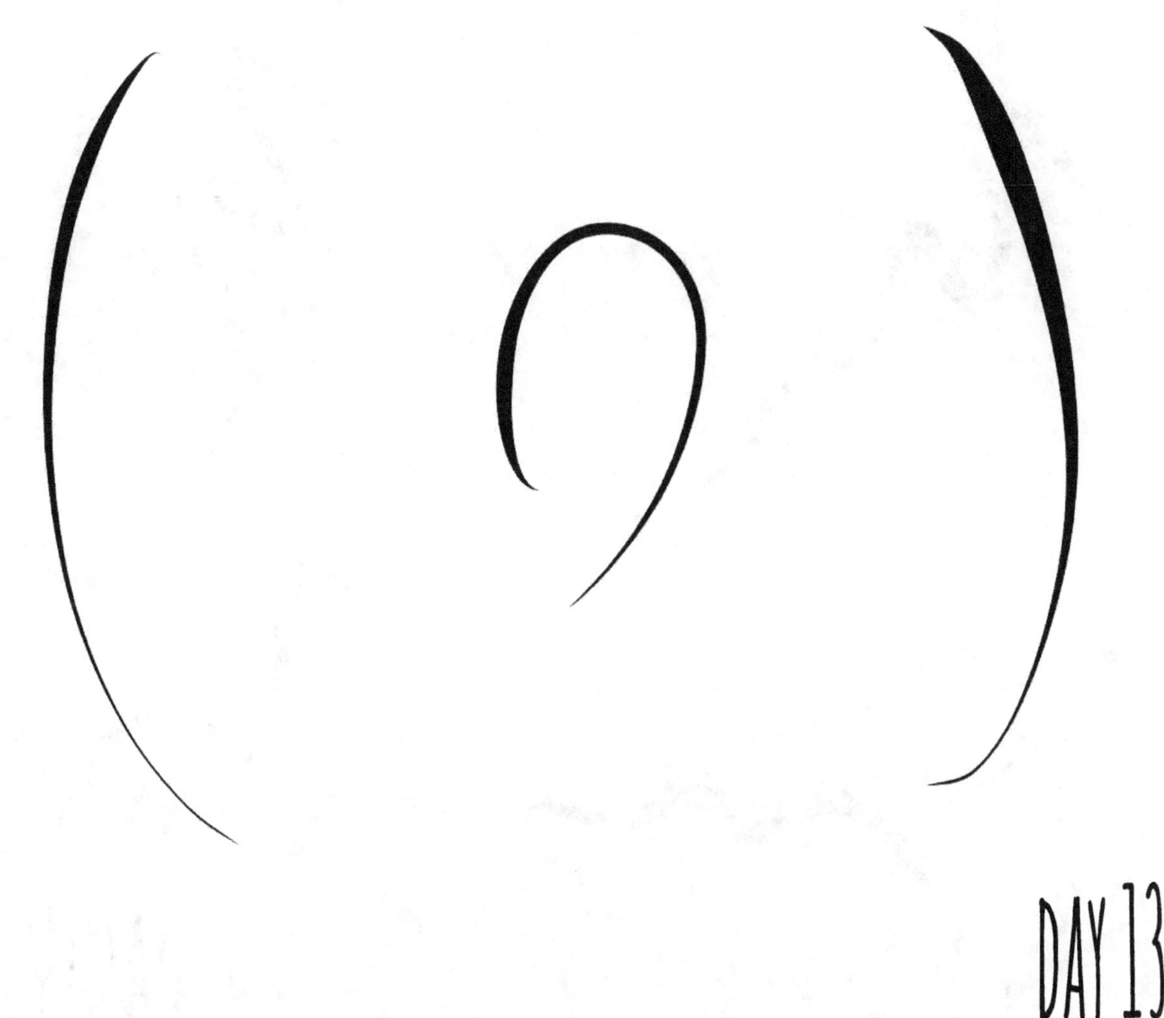

DAY 13

TO TRANSFORM A SCRIBBLE INTO SOMETHING AMAZING IT TAKES A LOT OF INNER THOUGHT.

AS YOU SIT QUIETLY IN SELF-REFLECTION WHAT DOES THIS SCRIBBLE TRANSFORM INTO?

DAY 14

DOESN'T THIS SCRIBBLE LOOK JUST LIKE A ___________
(ANIMAL)

SITTING UNDERNEATH ___________?
(TYPE OF PLANT)

DAY 15

HAS A SCRIBBLE EVER SPARKED YOUR IMAGINATION ABOUT A FUN MEMORY FROM THE PAST?

LET'S TURN THIS SCRIBBLE INTO A HAPPY MEMORY FROM A PLACE YOU WENT AS A KID.

DAY 16

It's important to be able to stop and smell the flowers in order to relax.

What flower can we turn these scribbles into?

DAY 17

USING YOUR IMAGINATION A SCRIBBLE CAN TURN YOU INTO WHATEVER YOU WANT TO BE. I CAN IMAGINE MYSELF SURFING A GIANT WAVE WITH MY PET SHARK.

DRAW ME HANGING TEN DUDE!!!

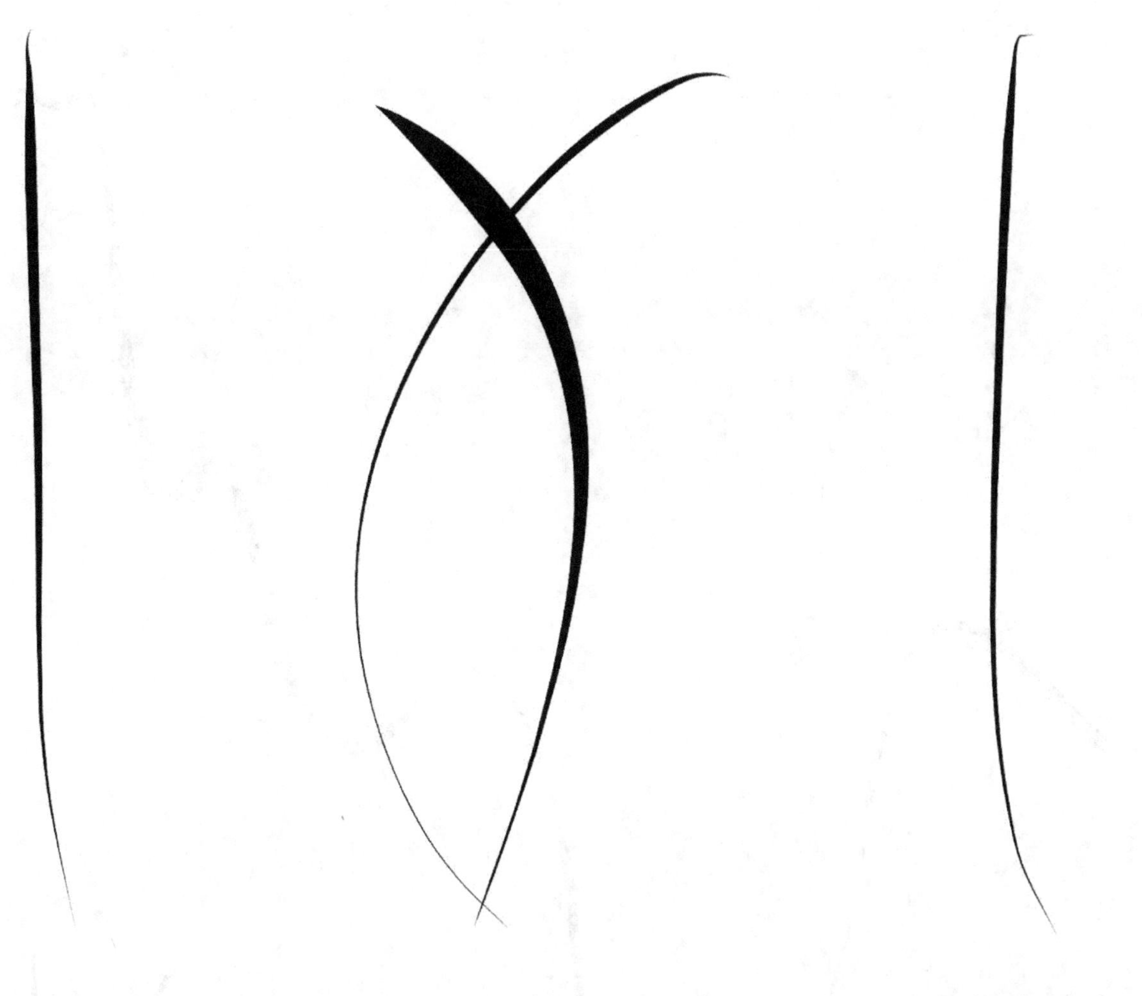

DAY 19

With a strong imagination a person can reach their goals in life.

Use your imagination to turn these scribbles into a far off place you would love to visit one day!

DAY 20

It can be a little scary using your imagination sometimes.

Use these scribbles to draw something spooky and scary.

DAY 21

WHEN I SEE THESE SCRIBBLES I PICTURE
TWO ____________
(PLURAL NOUN)
____________ IN THE ____________.
(PRESENT TENSE VERB)   (LOCATION)
CAN YOU DRAW IT FOR ME?

DAY 22

One of the best ways to start your day is with a boost of imagination!

Let's draw one thing you are hoping to do today?

DAY 23

USING YOUR IMAGINATION TO MAKE OTHERS FEEL
SPECIAL IS ONE OF THE GREATEST GIFTS WE HAVE.

CAN WE USE THESE SCRIBBLES TO DRAW SOMEONE
WE CARE ABOUT DOING A FUNNY ACTIVITY?
MAYBE WE CAN SHARE IT WITH THEM LATER.

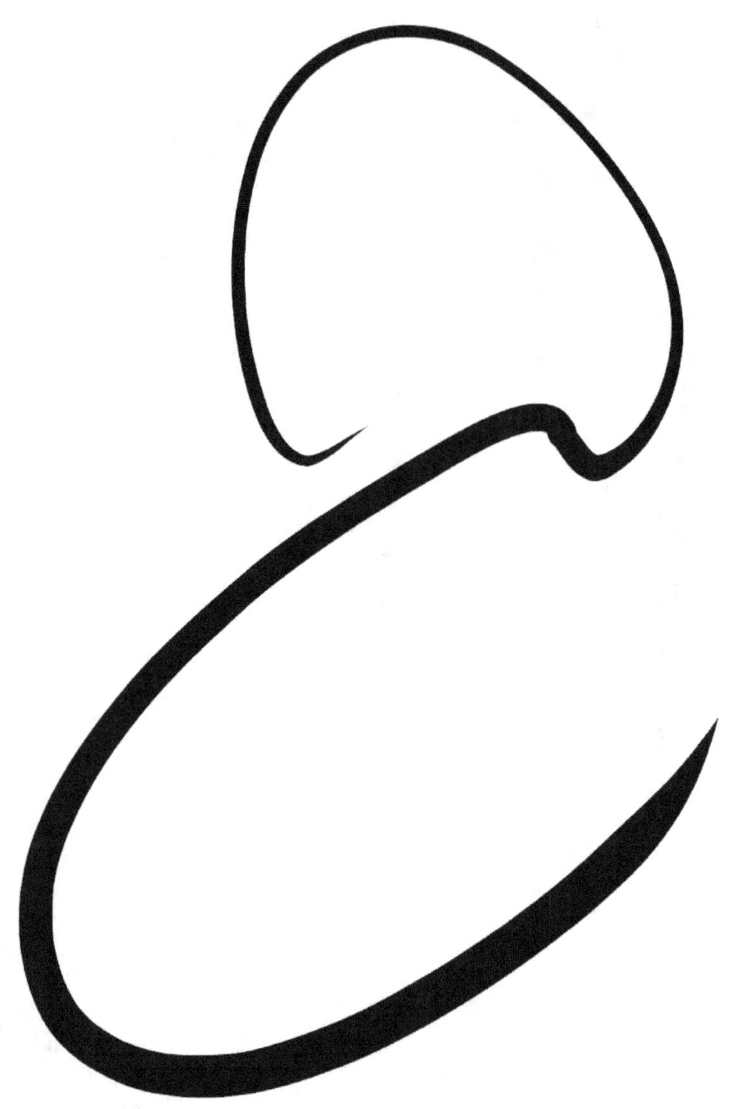

DAY 24

CAN YOU USE YOUR IMAGINATION TO DRAW WHAT
YOU SEE IN THIS SCRIBBLE AND TELL ME ABOUT IT?

DAY 25

SOMETIMES A GREAT IMAGINATION LEAVES GREAT IDEAS CRAWLING AROUND IN YOUR BRAIN LIKE A

__________.
(INSECT)

WHAT DO YOU HAVE CRAWLING AROUND IN YOUR BRAIN?

DAY 26

A DREAM IS YOUR IMAGINATION WORKING
OVERTIME WHILE YOU SLEEP.

COMPLETE THIS SCRIBBLE BY DRAWING ONE CRAZY
DREAM YOU CAN REMEMBER.

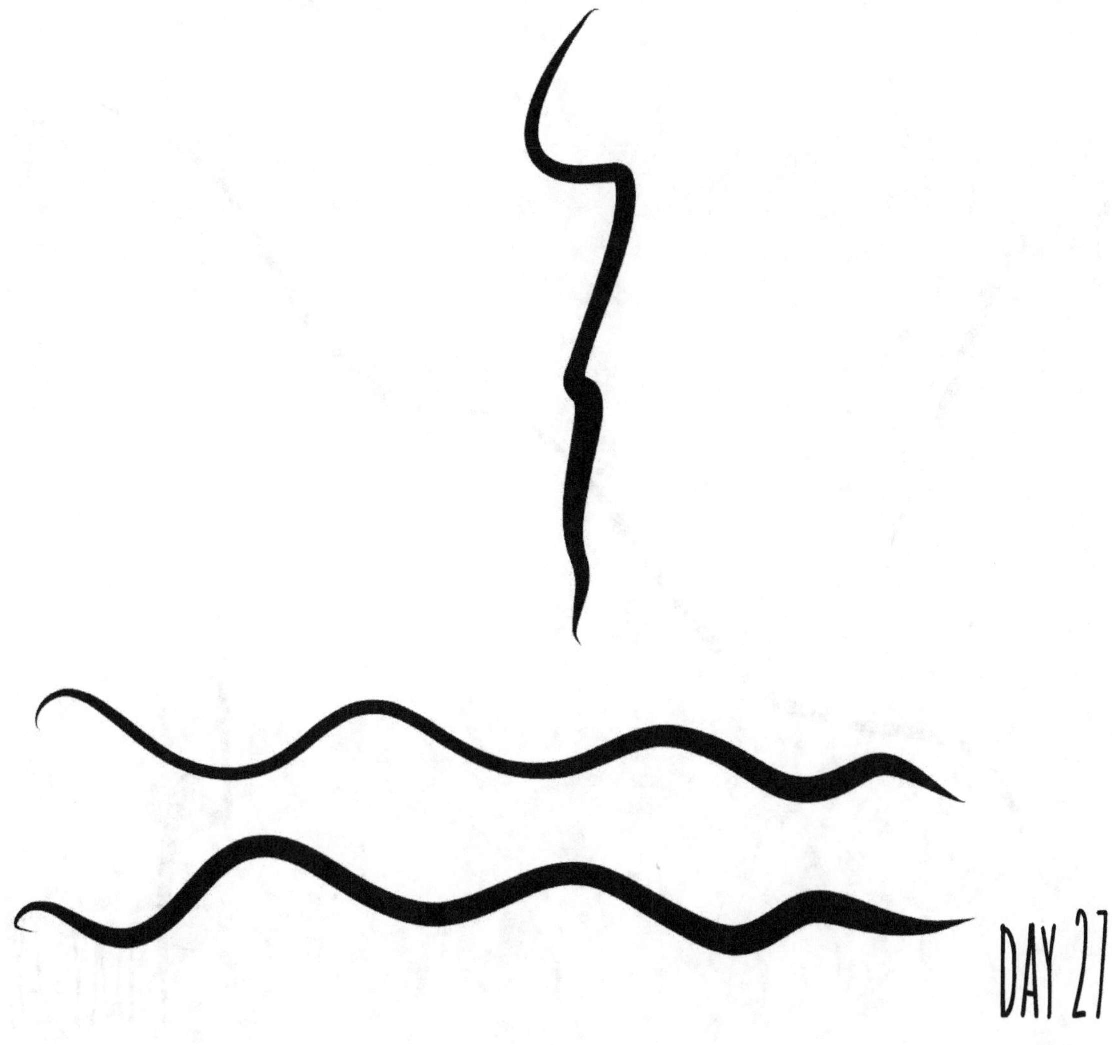

DAY 27

Can you use your imagination to turn these scribbles into something that makes your heart super happy?

Each day we should work to create our own picture of happiness in life.

SO FAR YOU HAVE DRAWN SOME SUPER PICTURES FROM YOUR SCRIBBLES. LET'S SEE HOW SUPER YOU ARE IN THIS DRAWING!

USE THESE SCRIBBLES TO CREATE YOUR SECRET SUPER ALTER EGO THAT NO ONE KNOWS.

DAY 29

DOES THIS SET OF SCRIBBLES LOOK EXACTLY LIKE A
________________ ________________ LOOKING AT BACK AT YOU?
(ADJECTIVE)   (NOUN)

HOW DOES THIS DRAWING MAKE YOU FEEL?

DAY 30

HOPEFULLY BY NOW YOUR IMAGINATION KNOWS NO BOUNDARIES! THE MOST BEAUTIFUL CREATIONS CAN SOMETIMES START FROM THE SIMPLEST PLACES.

WHAT BEAUTIFUL CREATION WILL THIS LINE BECOME?

DAY 31

www.ingramcontent.com/pod-product-compliance
Lightning Source LLC
Chambersburg PA
CBHW081408130726
47998CB00011B/3121